The Inside

A Collection

J. E. Mello

BookLeaf
Publishing

India | USA | UK

Made with ❤ on the BookLeaf Publishing Platform
www.bookleafpub.in
www.bookleafpub.com

Dedication

I'll never say your names, but I hope you see my love the same.

All that has changed is the start to love myself. I need more time.

Thank you, loves.

Preface

This is a collection of everything I hate to show. All of my hoarding and regret. I'm learning to stop apologizing. With this release, I can let go and clean this out. I won't ask you to enjoy this, only to spend time with one that you like. You can teach me about myself, after a while.

Acknowledgements

Thank you for believing in me,

Family, Jim, and every poet I met since birth.

1. Inside

The nerves are getting to me, I'm sorry.
Welcome in. I didn't have time to prepare for you.
Ignore the stallagtite rot above.
Everything is a mess, it's embarassing.

You can sit anywhere you want,
just away from my shadows.
Don't touch anything that's moving,
and don't ask any questions.

I'm sorry if I seem rude,
and don't mind the stains on teeth.
My design was more like yours,
I just failed to live up to it.

2. Mattress

simple fall
into crawl
arms are locked
strength to mock
shallow crate
suphocates
I could hear
family near
vibrant scream
enters scene
heartbeat coated
layers stoic
all would pass
all would laugh
I knew they'd calm
and I was wrong

3. I want to be a father

I was supposed to take care of the plants.
The soil was dried up.
I made sure to put the watering can close so I didn't
forget.
If my plants could wake me up, I could have saved them.
Did babies start to cry for fathers to care?
I should have put beady eyes on the top,
and replace their leaves with little arms for hugs.
I forgot to water them for months.
I should have put it in the middle of the room,
and make it follow me, wherever I go.
What if it taught me something new?
It was the easiest task of the day, watering plants.
If somebody reminded me, I could have saved them.
I want to be a father, one day.

4. Mad

Witness in time - my loves will
morph into jaguars.

They watch my shadow
slide on their plate - in my head

I hear them cackle
taking steps behind me - in my head

They sentenced me
to death before I spoke - in my head

I can feel their teeth
massaging my trachea - in my head

Even I will believe it.
My body knows,
and it's in my head,
already grown.

5. Drain

I want...

scabs in piles, picked from nails, and
acid pumped along the side with
little hairs and skin that give
the unbecoming smells of less.

The sewer system connects our asses;
spit and cum and shit as one.
Filter out my waste and piss so
I can be real...

I appreciate you, plumber and waste management.

6. Words

Words will crash against the seal;
letters may slip between our teeth,
but we snuff its meaning out like cigarettes.

Details will flash behind the words;
we can be tricked into giving life,
but all that is good shall be locked away.

Stories will grow along details;
this cancer can form in anyone,
but we use logic to dispel the magic.

Songs will break from the stories;
a lyric can swim in your head,
but it hasn't accrued your wealth.

Hope can dance near these songs,
but there is no reason to fear;
the seal will protect us.

7. Rapture

I am His soldier, and yet
the kingdom mourns me
gentile visions of peace
the exodus upon earth
angels deafen our eyes
the sin of man overflows
death spills onto my feet
catharsis in deliverance

8. Fury

Order,

- sit with spine up
- Ignore temptations
- Balanced meal
- Two weeks notice
- Flatter acquaintance
- Ignore history
- Greet bitch with staring problem
- Add electrolytes
- Ignore text from thieves
- Pay bill on time
- Ignore the gun on their hip
while they protect a second half
of pasters talking down but
using kids innocence and
freedom fighters turn to mince from
drones and ghosts with no intent to
hurt another life. Oh, shit,
and I'm supposed to smile through this?

It'll be right out. take a seat.

9. Stones

Victory will never be a gift.
    Apathy has us surrounded.
        Time is only a battleground.
We prayed to make our country work.
    But God already knew us.
        Nothing came from hope.
Do things right, and be polite.
    Work hard like your father said.
        Your nightmares may not come true.
But the evil that inhabits
    don't remember the stepping stones,
        though we are familiar by our teeth.

10. Birth

I made an observation.

(When did strangers tilting their heads mean something bad?)

(When did I first try to straighten my hair?)

(When did I become too loud in the theater?)

(When did I start to draw my portrait with skin color?)

(When did I start explaining the truth like it was my job?)

(When did the beads in her hair stop reminding me of marbles?)

It's impossible to be born Black.

11. Collaboration

This victim showed me a scar
where my shirt was.
This child hasn't found home.
This cup still has water in it.
This bottle has dust on its cap.
This dog keeps barking.
This lipstick dried up.
This hand isn't trembling, anymore.
This calendar is old.
This door wasn't locked.
This car vent smells weird.
This comforting hand lied.
This abuser apologized
to the wrong victim.

12. Childlike Fears

My loneliness is terrorism.
Acetaminophen nullifies a tear or two.
Love flourishes when you close your eyes.
Wives that loathe the ride home.
Husband on vacation, and he avoids a camera or two.
It's like television, a fleeting lie
that may never burst from your skin.
Kiss a new set of skin,
and purge the phone number or two.
She will never know. He will never know.
Happiness in spite of mundane.
Excite your dying brain.
A newly-scented drug or two.
You'll forget. You'll forget.

I wanted back to childlike fears.
My children danced around a hill of ants.
Stomping, cheers like colliseums. A headless doll rests
beside me.

13. To Be A Whore

Envious thoughts before I love all:

To be a whore is to endure;
A therapy of one-thousand degrees;
Burnout hearts before it's smart;
Deny one storm to keep things warm.

they're forced to digest shame.
    mine sits on the plate.
a roller coaster leads.
    I want to catch a ride.

Better. Now, I love you. Too.

14. Post-Relational Clarity

Listen to my rejection before you touch
and the allure of compassion seduces me.

Your connection made me feel safe,
while memories forgot to warn.

I know this rut comfortably,
but you will see my mind with disgust.

Leave confused because I won't let you know.

15. Funeral Speech

Be honest about my transgressions.
If I hurt you, don't let my eyes wander.
Guide my hands to cover your wounds.
Keep your smiles for when you're safe.
We can match our expectations.

//

There is no love for those you leech.
They were desperate for any embrace,
and your vampirism was just enough.
You justify a garden of ivy, clothing the rashes before
your eyes see.

//

My dearest,
Thank you for helping me.
I know this is a forever thing.
Anyone can say they'll die for you,
I chose to live for us both.
Even if you don't benefit,
I'll be there, devoted to your love.

My mind recreates a life with you alone.

//   16

You speak to me in a kind loving way,
to heal me and my toxic love.
You value art and people's stories.
You're sensitive and you care so fucking much.
I still think about you, time to time.
Don't come back, love.

16. Familiar Faces

you're just like the woman who hates me.
her eyes avoided mine like that.
a knife without a plate.
oh, even the same threats.
she had a different style,
like she'd stop loving me, too.
shit.
poor girl.

you're just like the man who hates me.
his fist was tightened like that.
a meandered grin to entertain.
ah, that same tearful goodbye.
he used different words:
"nobody will ever respect you.
fuck you."
poor guy.

17. Lakes

Your friend is drifting by.
His flesh familiar, past bacteria.
The eyes are hollowed out.

The muscles cling to bone.
Waves splash red, and fish look fed.
His last words were a curse.

You loved his lack of violence.
All was fun, until a gun
made him a hypocrite!

18. Tasteless

appetizers without a tongue
object in the empty
betrayed wisdom twice
targeted laughter muted
statistics damned eternal
acidic rejection twice
reflection checkpoint denial
numbed before regret
careless
again

19. Empty

to live is beyond existence.
This is not.

to want is joyless harlotry.
This existence is not.

to hate is passion at a dam.
This existence is not to.

to cry is to feel, want, lose.
This existence is simply not to.

Focus on the one who struggles. This is a memory of
limbs falling in a pit of empty regret.
I submit now; This existence is simply not to try.

20. Flies

Filth is a reminder.
Biology's remission.
The mites chew my fear
of endlessness when decaying.

Quiet.

I stopped scrubbing.
But my infection never came.
Now I swat the flies
to convince them I'm alive.

21. Feeling

I didn't enjoy the pain, but I was thrilled that I could withstand it.

Satan's claws pulled at my nerves. Blood and ink danced with each other just below me.

The apparitions plagued my lungs and displaced my heart.

Moments I felt the space without light, screaming with a closed throat.

I felt too alive. One spike impaled me, and pained over a thousand cuts.

Every movement, a blank check of hurt cast into the crematorium.

How glorious it is to feel.